Panorama-Books: GEORGIA

With thirty-three color plates

HANS W. HANNAU

GEORGIA

Distributed by

DOUBLEDAY & COMPANY, INC.
GARDEN CITY, NEW YORK

Wrapper and cover designed by Gerhard M. Hotop

Library of Congress Catalog Card Number 68–19348
Wilhelm Andermann Verlag, Munich
Printed in Germany. 168

A Bird's-Eye View of Georgia's History

It is commonly believed that the Creek and Cherokee Indians were the indigenous inhabitants of the area known today as Georgia. Actually they were preceded by earlier "civilizations" that date back thousands of years before the Christian era. Ceremonial mounds, whose origins remain shrouded in mystery, are all that remain of those distant Georgian cultures.

Nevertheless, it was the Creek and Cherokee that Hernando de Soto discovered when he arrived here in 1540 – the first white man to set foot on Georgia soil. He was followed by French trappers and explorers and English freebooters, and each group, in concert with the Indians, harried the early Spanish establishments and missions. When General James Edward Oglethorpe arrived in 1733, the English formally undertook to challenge the position of Spain in the area.

Oglethorpe was a member of Parliament, a philanthropist, and a shrewd speculator. He helped to save many an Englishman from debtor's prison if the Englishman would consider being transported to the New World to assist in its colonization. In this endeavor, Oglethorpe was joined by flocks of Protestant refugees escaping persecution on the European mainland. Later, a more cultivated class of adventurers received large land grants in the new territory of Georgia as an inducement to come to America.

Politically, George II planned that this new area, under English settlement, should be a buffer between the Spanish forces in Florida and the established English colonies to the north of Georgia. From 1739 to 1742, many a skirmish took place between Spanish and English colonial forces, until the English achieved a decisive victory in the Battle of Bloody Marsh on St. Simon Island in 1742. The threat of Spanish invasion of Georgia was removed forever.

By 1754, the colony was sufficiently advanced to become a royal province, with a governor and a two-chamber legislature. And by 1766, there were nearly 10,000 white people and 7,800 Negroes in the new territory. The Indians had begun their trek westward. The high cost of maintaining the colony forced the English to tax the colonists to defray expenses. This action was bitterly resented in Georgia, and "taxation without representation" became the rallying cry of discontent toward the mother country. It was not, however, until the Second Continental Congress convened that Georgia decided to participate in the rebellion. Three Georgians signed the Declaration of Independence – Button Gwinnett, Lyman Hall, and George Walton.

In 1778 the British attacked Georgia. Savannah was captured first, and by 1779 every important town in Georgia had been taken by the British. Nevertheless, the rebels kept up a constant guerrilla warfare, harassing the British to the point where much brutality and bloodshed were caused by both sides. At the war's end, extensive land grants were awarded to the revolutionary veterans. The property of hundreds of loyalists was confiscated, and many loyalists left Georgia because of the hostile sentiment of the former revolutionaries. Georgia became the fourth state to ratify the Constitution of the United States.

In 1793, Eli Whitney invented the cotton gin in Georgia. This invention was to affect the economic structure of the South drastically, and the political life of the country as a whole. Slavery, which had been dying out in Georgia, now became more important than ever as more cotton was planted. Slaves were needed in increasing numbers for the cultivation of large plantations.

The population of the state had doubled by 1800. In forty years it was five times the size – almost 700,000. With the new prosperity, railroads came to Georgia. Prosperity rested mainly on the larger cotton plantations, which in turn depended on slave labor.

The problem of the extension of slave territory – on the basis of which the

Republican Party had come into existence – was beginning to divide the nation. With Lincoln's election in 1860, Georgia felt that it had no option but to secede from the Union. For almost three years there was little fighting in Georgia during the Civil War, but in 1864 General Sherman's forces approached Atlanta, occupying it on September 2. On November 14, Sherman set fire to the city and then set out on his historic march to the sea. It is estimated that the value of property destroyed en route amounted to more than $ 100,000,000. By the end of December, Sherman had occupied Savannah. It is now known that there was a strong movement for peace in Georgia before Sherman moved into the state, and when a new federal army appeared in the west, the state surrendered its forces.

At the end of the war the economic structure of Georgia lay shattered. The state had lost three quarters of its wealth and countless lives.

The Negro was guaranteed full political dignity under the Fourteenth Amendment to the Constitution. Georgia refused to ratify the amendment, and Congress placed the state under military rule. Thirty-two Negroes were elected to the legislature, the Fourteenth Amendment was ratified, and the federal troops departed. During the Reconstruction Era, Georgia took on new importance as an industrial state, forging commercial and economic links with the North. The scars of the civil struggle were fast fading.

Although Georgia retains an important rural and agricultural segment to its economy, its industrialization has become legendary. The major city, Atlanta, is enjoying fantastic prosperity as the rail, air, and communications center of the entire Southeast. Other Georgia cities, too, are having an unprecedented boom.

The Beauties of Georgia

The loveliness of Georgia is as varied as its terrain. In the north are the magnificent

Appalachian Mountains; in the northwest are the elongated plateaus and more mountains. The northwest corner of Georgia is so cut off from the rest of the state by mountains that it failed to secede before the Civil War. It is still called "the Free State of Dade" by old-timers. Central Georgia is the famous Piedmont region. To the east are the long coastal plain and the Sea Islands. Brunswick is fourteen feet above sea level, but parts of Georgia rise to a height of almost 4800 feet.

Georgia is the largest state east of the Mississippi, having an area of 59,265 square miles. It is bordered on the west by Alabama, on the south by Florida, on the southeast by the Atlantic Ocean, and on the north and northeast by Tennessee, North Carolina, and South Carolina. The coast of Georgia stretches for almost a hundred miles and is fringed by the Sea Islands, which are separated from the mainland by lagoons, narrow channels, and sounds – all navigable by small craft.

The Appalachian range of northern Georgia is made up of the Blue Ridge Mountains and a continuation of the Smoky Mountains. This area is scantily populated, because it is generally inaccessible and good agricultural land is rather scarce.

The state's larger cities are situated in the Piedmont region of middle Georgia. This is generally rolling land, where an occasional thousand-foot-high mountain is a rather conspicuous geographical feature, like Stone Mountain near Atlanta and Kennesaw Mountain near Marietta. The Chattahoochee River runs through this section of the state, and the Savannah River is the boundary between Georgia and South Carolina.

The coastal plain of Georgia constitutes the entire southern half of the state. It contains, among other places of interest, the famous Okefenokee Swamp, the second-largest fresh-water swamp in the United States.

Above and beyond all these variations of topography, Nature has bestowed a mild and healthy climate on Georgia, where long summers and short winters prevail. Although the weather is colder in the mountains, as one would expect, subtropical conditions exist along the Florida line. Consequently, Georgia has both winter and summer resorts. The mountains are delightful for summer vacationers, and the southern part of the state, low and warm, has an ideal winter climate.

With the generally beneficent climate goes an exceptional variety of flora. Pine, oak, elm, cedar, sycamore, and poplar are ubiquitous. The red maple displays everywhere the glories of its scarlet leaves and red buds. In the wooded areas of the state are hickory, persimmon, black gum, sweet gum – and the tulip tree, with its pale flowers. Moss-draped live oak flourishes on the coast, hemlock in the mountain areas. Of course, the South would not be the South without the magnolia tree and its heavy-scented, creamy blossoms. The chinaberry tree grows mostly in fence rows and in the yards of tenant farmers, and the spreading mimosa with its powder-puff blossoms and lacy foliage is still found, though much reduced in numbers by a blight a few years ago. Pink and white dogwood bloom in the spring and add more color to an already colorful state.

There are apple orchards and pecan arbors in the foothills, and peach trees in central Georgia. In the south, the slash pine is valuable for papermaking and is a source of turpentine. Woodland covers almost two thirds of the state, and Georgia is eleventh among the states in lumber production (chiefly pine) and third in pulpwood. The harder varieties of wood are found in the northeastern counties.

Georgia's flower is the Cherokee Rose, a deliciously fragrant white blossom with a yellow center. Roses bloom almost everywhere. The daffodil, crocus, forsythia, and marigold grow abundantly in gardens, while honeysuckle, blue iris, yellow jasmine, and pink and yellow primroses grow wild throughout the countryside.

Better Homes and Gardens of Georgia

The picturesque landscape of Georgia seemed to call out for homes that would blend with the natural beauty of the state and even enhance it.

Wattle-and-daub huts prevailed in the early years of settlement, followed by the utilitarian log cabins. Sometimes a log cabin was placed beside another and the two were covered with a single roof, which allowed for a breezeway between the houses. This was the origin of today's breezeway.

As time went by, the log cabins were replaced by clapboard houses, particularly in Savannah. Because the economic development of Georgia did not come until the 1800's, there were few Georgian-colonial homes of distinction. Nevertheless, during the colonial period, when frontier cabins were still being built along the Cherokee frontier, a simple but pleasing type of native architecture developed along the Atlantic Coast, particularly in Savannah and Augusta. Over a high basement – which usually was the first story – was built a small frame house. To reach the main entrance on the second floor required a straight flight of steps. The roof projected over a porch lined with slender wooden columns. In the country, the porch was carried all along the front. A fine example is Wild Heron House, near Savannah, built by Francis Harris in 1756 and believed to be the oldest plantation house in Georgia.

The era that followed was the Federal Period, in which the influence of English Regency was very strong. This style, however, blended with earlier Georgian colonial to create buildings that combined the best features of both. The Blount House near Macon is typical of this type of architecture. A number of beautiful Federal houses were built in Savannah during the opening decades of the nineteenth century, designed by the English architect William Jay. These houses reflect the elegance of Bath, England, a famous watering spot in the eighteenth and early nineteenth centuries. Outstanding examples are the Telfair Academy, the Richardson-Owen House, and the Scarborough House – in Savannah.

With the advent of the great cotton plantations and the enormous prosperity of the landowners, an interest developed in the classical architectural details of ancient Greece. Houses were built in the style called Greek Revival, the characteristic feature of which was the two-story colonnade of four, five, or six columns supporting a front pediment.

Broad verandahs and high ceilings were provided, well suited to the long hot summers. The style quickly spread to the cities, and throughout the entire state arose spacious columned homes that contributed vastly to the great antebellum traditions.

There are many outstanding examples of Greek Revival, one of them being the Old Executive Mansion in Milledgeville. Variations of the style, with porticoes bearing two galleries and superimposed columns, are also found, as in the Williams-Ferguson House in the same city.

During the latter part of the Greek Revival period, the Gothic Revival came to Georgia. This was a blend of Gothic and Classical Roman and Greek styles, where elaborate dormered dwellings with steep roofs blended with the gingerbread and jigsaw extravagances of the 1880's.

Building in Georgia had come to a halt during the Civil War, but by the 1880's the more progressive centers were able to fall in line with the new French Renaissance style, which had come to the North ten years earlier. Some of the older houses on Peachtree Street in Atlanta, which featured mansard roofs, are examples of this style.

Although Georgia's production of marble is second only to that of Vermont, there always has been rather little use of the stone in building. Much preferred is the beautiful yellow pine of Georgia, which has proved to be strong and durable.

The Cities of Georgia

Atlanta

The capital of Georgia is Atlanta, the principal city of the state. Rich in history, it is also representative of the "New South." General Sherman had burned Atlanta to the ground during the Civil War. In the century since, Atlanta has emerged as the leading industrial metropolis of the Southeast.

Atlanta's founding, in 1837, was due to the foresight and enterprise of pioneer railroad men. Originally known as Terminus and later as Marthasville, in honor of the governor's daughter, Martha Lumpkin, Atlanta was selected as the railroad junction of the Georgia Railroad and the Western & Atlantic line (Atlanta is the feminine form of Atlantic). So important did this site become that Atlanta was incorporated as a city in 1847.

During the Civil War, Atlanta was a strategic supply and communications center for the Confederacy. Heavy fortifications twelve miles in length surrounded the city, but it was not until 1864 that the war arrived. Three battles were fought in July of that year – the Battle of Peachtree Creek, the Battle of Atlanta, and the Battle of Ezra Church – and the besieged city lay in ruins. On September 2, the mayor formally surrendered Atlanta to the Union Army. General Sherman thereupon ordered the evacuation of the city and put it to the torch. He resumed his march toward the sea and Savannah, having destroyed all but 400 of Atlanta's 4500 houses and commercial buildings.

At the end of the war, Atlanta's citizens returned to commence the arduous task of reconstruction. In 1868, the city was designated as the state capital.

After a century of rapid and untiring progress, Atlanta teems with some 1550 industrial plants manufacturing over 3500 products, among them aircraft, autos, textiles, chemicals, food, and iron and steel products. The city has nineteen institutions of higher learning, among which are the Georgia Institute of Technology and Emory and Oglethorpe Universities.

There are more than a hundred parks in Atlanta, many of which are in their natural state. Notable is *Piedmont Park,* in the northern part of Atlanta, covering 185 acres of rolling, tree-dotted land, a lake, a golf course, and recreational fields. The *Peace Monument* at the 14th Street entrance is a bronze figure of the Goddess of Peace holding out an olive branch to a kneeling Confederate soldier.

Not far away is the Atlanta Memorial Center, built in memory of Georgians who died in a plane crash in Paris in June 1963. This gleaming white building includes a big art gallery, a symphony hall seating 1850, and a theater seating 850.

In the northern section are the campuses of *Oglethorpe* and *Georgia Tech Universities*. At Oglethorpe, a vault called the *Crypt of Civilization* has been built under the Administration Building to preserve materials illustrative of our modern era. The *Georgia Institute of Technology* has more than 7500 students studying in eighteen schools of engineering, science, management, and architecture. It is important also for its nuclear research.

In the Druid Hills Section of northeastern Atlanta is *Emory University* and the *Emory University Museum*, which houses an Egyptian and Babylonian collection of mummies traceable to 7000 B.C. In the Theology Building is a collection of memorabilia of John Wesley, the eighteenth-century founder of Methodism. Its medical school has the fascinating Yerkes experimental laboratory.

Notable also is the *Atlanta University* complex of five colleges, one of the foremost Negro educational centers in the United States.

The *Oakland Cemetery* is situated in the southeastern part of the city. Here Margaret Mitchell, author of *Gone with the Wind,* is buried. Here, too, is the *Confederate Monument,* a 65-foot granite shaft dedicated to the unknown dead of the Civil War, of which several thousand are buried in the cemetery.

The 144 acres of *Grant Park* are the city's loveliest. The park contains a zoo and many recreational facilities. Among the notable attractions is the *Cyclorama,* housed in the Cyclorama Building. One of the three largest paintings in the world, the Cyclorama is 50 feet high and 400 feet around and weighs 18,000 pounds. It reproduces the Battle of Atlanta (July 22, 1864) in detail.

The *Wren's Nest* is the former home of Joel Chandler Harris, creator of Uncle Remus and Br'er Rabbit. This irregularly shaped building is furnished much as it was during the author's lifetime and is maintained by the Uncle Remus Memorial Association.

Last but not least is the eighteen-million-dollar Atlanta stadium, which drew one

13

and a half million visitors in 1967 to see football, baseball, and soccer. Atlanta is big league: the Falcons, the Braves, and the Chiefs call it home.

Augusta

Overlooking the Savannah River is Augusta, a serene and gracious city of old houses and flowered parkways. Its mild winters attract tourists from far and wide, and its nationally known as a smart winter resort.

Fort Augusta was founded in 1735 by James Oglethorpe. From 1785 to 1795 it was the capital of Georgia, and it was here that the Constitution was ratified by the state.

As cotton began to supplant tobacco in the economy of Georgia, Augusta took the lead as a market for this new product. One of Eli Whitney's first cotton gins was set up here, and progress continued apace, only momentarily held up by fearful yellow-fever epidemics in 1840 and 1854, which took countless human lives. Augusta escaped the destruction occasioned by Sherman's march to the sea and was not occupied by Union troops until after Lee's surrender in 1865.

Augusta is still a large cotton market. It is also an important textile-manufacturing city and the leading producer of clay products in the Southeast. As a resort city, it offers unlimited opportunities for recreation. There are four splendid golf courses, including the Augusta National Golf Club, famous for the Masters Invitation Tournaments, and many facilities for horseback riding and polo.

Among the places of interest in Augusta are the *Site of Fort Augusta*, marked by a Celtic cross, at the foot of which lies one of Oglethorpe's original cannons; the *Signers Monument*, a fifty-foot-high granite shaft rising from the center of a green that honors the three signers of the Declaration of Independence (two are buried here, George Walton and Lyman Hall. The burial place of Button Gwinnett, who was killed in a duel, has never been discovered); the *First Presbyterian Church*, built in 1812, where Woodrow Wilson's father was a pastor for a time; *Meadow Garden,* which was the home of George Walton (George Washington was entertained in Meadow Garden in 1791, and Lafayette in 1825. It is now a museum of the Daughters of the American Revolution); *Mackay House,* the oldest house in Augusta, erected in 1760 (thirteen American patriots were hanged here during the Revolution by order of the British commander); *the Clark Hill Dam and Reservoir,* twenty-two miles above Augusta, which impounds a vast reservoir with an irregular 1000-mile wooded shoreline along the Georgia-South Carolina state border (fishing, boating, and hunting are permitted in certain sections and are designated as recreation sites).

Athens

Athens is the largest city in the rolling hills of the Piedmont area of north-western Georgia. It owes much of its prosperity to the presence of the University of Georgia and is a complex of research facilities and plants manufacturing textiles, plastics, metals, dairy foods, and paper products.

Athens is a city of fine antebellum homes exemplifying the Greek Revival architecture of which the South is so fond. Greek porticoes with pediments and large Doric columns are dominant architectural features. Boxwood gardens and magnolia blooms embody the romantic traditions of the deep South. *The Ross Crane House,* built in 1842, is one of the finest structures in this style.

The University of Georgia is of particular importance and interest. Chartered in 1785, it is the oldest state-chartered university in the country. Its enrollment has increased from a handful of students at its beginning to more than 15,000 today.

A local curiosity is a double-barreled cannon – the only one in the world – designed for use in the Civil War. It never worked, because the barrels could not be synchronized. Another curiosity is the *Tree That Owns Itself.* This is a white oak to which was bequeathed in 1820 all the land within eight feet of its trunk. The enclosure is encircled by chains to ensure that no harm comes to the tree.

Macon

Macon is the Old South from a cultural standpoint, the New South when one considers its economic progress. It is a comfortable, unhurried city, full of beauty. Even the downtown area has parkways planted in roses, crape myrtle, and palmettos.

The development of Macon, situated almost in the dead center of the state, began when the Indians ceded all the land between the Oconee and Ocmulgee Rivers in 1802, 1804, and 1805 to the state. Fort Hawkins was constructed in 1806 to protect the state against Indian insurrection, and the modern settlement of Macon stems from this date. (A reproduction of the original fort is open to the public.)

The fertility of the soil attracted pioneers and tradespeople, who founded the city, naming it after Nathaniel Macon, a prominent North Carolina statesman. During the Civil War, Macon was the temporary state capital after Milledgeville fell into Sherman's hands. Jefferson Davis was brought to Macon after his capture at Irwinsville.

Macon is known to thousands of soldiers of World War II who received their training at Camp Harris and Wheeler nearby.

Wesleyan College, the first college in the world chartered to grant degrees to women, is situated here. Opened in 1839, Wesleyan has become very popular with foreign-born Methodists, among whom were the Soong sisters (one of whom became Mme. Chiang Kai-shek).

Macon contains the home of Sidney Lanier, Georgia's best-known poet (1842–1881). He had been a prisoner of the war in the North, where he contracted lung trouble and died at the age of thirty-nine.

The Hay House is a splendid twenty-four-room antebellum villa of Italian Renaissance architecture.

Baconsfield Park has 117 acres of natural forest, picnic areas, botanical gardens, tennis courts, and other play facilities.

Particularly attractive are the suburban sections of Macon, where there is an assortment of fine antebellum houses and examples of the most modern architecture.

Savannah, with Independent Presbyterian Church in background

IN HONOR OF THE
CONFEDERATE SOLDIERS
WHO DIED TO REPEL
UNCONSTITUTIONAL
INVASION TO PROTECT THE
RIGHTS RESERVED TO THE
PEOPLE TO PERPETUATE
FOR EVER THE SOVEREIG
OF THE STATES

Confederate War Memorial, Brunswick

*ral
B. Gordon
ument
Capitol Building,
nta*

Spring in Georgia (Blue Ridge)

Double-barreled cannon, Athens

Atlanta sky

Confederate memorial carving on Stone Mountain

Fort Pulaski National Monument

Into the Okefenokee Swamp, Waycro.

Midway Church

Pierce Butler Plantation, Darien

Spanish moss at Wormsloe Plantation, Isle of Hope

National Cemetery,
Andersonville

Mountain sc
near
Young Harr

*Birthplace
of Georgia's
foremost poet,
Sidney Lanier,
Macon*

In the mountains near Clayton

Country church (Harmony Baptist Church) near Blue Ridge

St. Simon's Isla
the Old Christ (
(1736)

Savannah Beach

The Juliette Gordon Low birthplace, Savannah

Fort Frederica

Very few cities dispute with Savannah the title of the most beautiful and historic city in the South. Built on a walled bluff overlooking the Savannah River, sixteen miles from the Atlantic, Savannah is the birthplace of the Georgia colony and is the second-largest city in the state. Cognizant of its gracious way of life, Savannah nevertheless fosters the progress and tempo of contemporary living in its role of thriving industrial seaport.

Because of its proximity to the Atlantic, snow and ice are strangers here. Summer heat is tempered by the ocean breezes, and several resort areas, including Savannah Beach and Wilmington Island, are nearby.

James Oglethorpe and a group of English settlers landed here in 1733. He laid out a plan of the town that provided living space for 240 families, making Savannah one of the first planned cities in the United States. Savannah probably was named after the Sawana or Shawnee Indians, who once inhabited the river valley, although some historians claim that it comes from the Spanish word *sabana,* meaning flat country, which had been applied to the whole area by the Spanish explorers two centuries earlier.

During the next few years, Spanish, Portuguese, and German Jews plus English and Scottish immigrants greatly increased the original population. Among the newcomers were Charles and John Wesley, founders of the Methodist movement.

During the Revolution, Savannah was a most important seaport; it was captured by the British in 1778 and held until 1782. General Pulaski was killed in an attempt to wrest the city from British occupation.

Savannah was the site of a Confederate navy yard and an important supply point during the Civil War. Since it was destined to be the terminal point of Sherman's march to the sea, the city was evacuated just before his arrival to protect it from bombardment.

Savannah's prosperity has always been measured by the activity of its port. It has today more than three hundred industrial plants and is the center of the expanding Southern pulp and paper business. Through its splendid harbor pass a variety of products – petroleum, sugar, lumber, cotton, naval stores, peanuts, fertilizers, and tobacco, to name but a few.

But with all its commercial success, Savannah maintains its individual charm, which arises from its historic and cultural heritage. Savannah's cuisine, especially seafood, is famous, and large, leisurely dinners are served at two o'clock in the afternoon. Sailing parties are common. Many other customs, too, provide the city with a quality of graciousness and sophistication. Charming also are Savannah's cobblestoned riverfront, the broad avenues, and the many old squares shaded by majestic oaks. One of the city's most picturesque residential areas is found in the Old Fort Section near the river. Six city blocks have been restored on the site of what was once the famous Old Trustee's Garden, the first experimental garden in America. Here are the oldest house in Savannah, the Herb Shop, and the Pirate's House, a restaurant associated with Stevenson's *Treasure Island*.

Space allows mention of only a few of the many historic sites in Savannah.

The *Owen-Thomas House*, designed by William Jay, is an excellent example of Regency architecture and contains authentic antiques of the period. Lafayette was a guest here in 1825.

Telfair Academy of Arts and Sciences occupies the site of the Royal Governor's Mansion. Built about 1820 by William Jay, it is a fine example of Classical Revival architecture. The museum contains Renaissance and modern paintings, textiles, period furniture, and traveling exhibits.

Factors Walk is situated on the riverfront between River and Bay Streets and was the commercial center of the town in the early nineteenth century. The various buildings are two stories high on the Bay Street front and four stories high in the rear.

Johnson Square contains the grave of the revolutionary war hero General Nathanael Greene.

Christ Church dates from 1838. This church organized what is believed to be the first Protestant Sunday School in America.

The Intependent Presbyterian Church, founded in 1755, was designed after St. Martin's-in-the-Fields, Trafalgar Square, London. It has a beautiful steeple and a lovely Georgian interior.

Forsyth Park was laid out in 1851 and contains a fountain resembling the one on the Place de la Concorde in Paris. It is particularly beautiful in early spring, during the azalea season.

A word should be added here about *Savannah Beach* and the adjoining *Sea Islands* of Georgia. *Savannah Beach* extends along the edge of historic *Tybee Island*, at the mouth of the Savannah River. There is a fine ocean beach and a lighthouse, the original of which dates back to 1736.

The Islands

The beautiful semitropical islands that extend along the Georgia coast from the Florida border to St. Catherine's Sound were inhabited as long ago as 2500 B.C. Spain maintained missions and garrisons here in the sixteenth and seventeenth centuries. English warships rendezvoused at Gascoigne Bluff in 1736, long before the islands were ceded to England in 1763. The notorious pirate Blackbeard is said to have hidden his treasure on Blackbeard Island.

St. Simon's Island is connected with many historical events, starting with the Anglo-Spanish Battle of Bloody March in 1742. Aaron Burr sought refuge here after he had killed Alexander Hamilton in a duel. John and Charles Wesley preached Methodism here in the town of Frederica.

On the western side of the island is *Fort Frederica National Monument*, where the foundations of many of the original homes of the Oglethorpe era (1736–1749) have been uncovered. There are opportunities for picnicking, fishing, boating, and swimming.

Sea Island is a delightful all-year resort in a splendid setting of palms and pines. There is a five-mile-long beach and facilities for golf, skeet shooting, horseback riding, tennis, and fishing.

Jekyll Island, once the retreat of millionaires, is now a state-owned public park, which is reached from the mainland by a causeway. Its main attraction is the magnificent beach – nine and one half miles long and three hundred feet wide. The swimming is superb, and paved roads make all parts of the island accessible. A wildlife refuge is maintained here.

Columbus

Columbus was the last frontier town of the thirteen original colonies. Constructed as a trading post on the western Georgian border, it became the only state-conceived community in Georgia when the governor, in 1827, asked the state engineers to plan the city here.

The city lies on the east bank of the Chattahoochee River, at the foot of a series of powerful falls. Streets are wide and are laid out in an orderly pattern. Magnificent trees stand in wide grassy plots, and when spring brings the flowering white dogwood and lavendar wistaria, the whole city is a blaze of color.

During the Civil War, Columbus was an important depot for Confederate supplies. It was taken by Union troops in one of the last battles of the war, actually a week after Lee had surrendered.

Columbus is the South's second-largest textile center, but a variety of other industrial and commercial products are manufactured here as well.

Nine miles from the city is *Fort Benning*, which occupies a military reservation of 182,000 acres east and south of Columbus.

Columbus has a statue to Bragg Smith, a Negro, who lost his life trying to save the superintendent of public works from being crushed in a collapsing trench. The *Bragg*

Smith Monument stands in Porterdale Cemetery, an interesting Negro burial ground.

St. Elmo (1832) is a stately and historic two-story Greek Revival house, constructed of handmade brick molded by slaves on the premises. Twelve Doric columns, forty feet high, lend grace and dignity to the massive construction. Visitors to St. Elmo included Presidents Polk and Fillmore, Henry Clay, and the English novelist William Thackeray.

Columbus has a notable *Confederate Museum* on a gunboat, which was burned and sunk during the Civil War and recently salvaged and restored.

National Parks and Monuments

Andersonville is of historical interest because of the Confederate prison that was situated here during the Civil War. The horrors of the prison were graphically described in Mackinlay Kantor's Pulitzer Prize-winning novel *Andersonville*. More than one quarter of the 53,345 Union prisoners held here died from mistreatment and over-crowding. Henry Wirz, the prison superintendent, was hanged, in what was probably the first war crimes trial in history.

Chattahoochee and Oconee National Forests. These forests cover 677,000 acres in northern Georgia and more than 100,000 acres in central Georgia. They not only contribute to the state's vast timber production but also contain forty-two recreation areas for swimming, picnicking, camping, hunting in season, and fishing. In the Chattahoochee National Forests is Georgia's highest point – Brasstown Bald (4784 feet).

Chickamauga and Chattanooga National Military Park. This, the oldest and largest of the national military parks (8190 acres), extends into Tennessee as well as Georgia. The park commemorates several Civil War battles fought here for Chattanooga, the most important battlefield being Chickamauga, in Georgia.

Fort Pulaski National Monument. This monument stands at the mouth of the Savannah River. It is an irregular, pentagon-shaped building 1500 feet in circumference and is surrounded by a moat crossed by drawbridges. The massive structure took eighteen years to build (1829–1847), and its walls are seven to eleven feet thick. It took Union troops less than two days to capture the fort, however; they bombarded it for thirty hours, in 1862, and it surrendered. This effectively demonstrated the fact that old-type fortifications could not withstand modern weaponry and were outdated.

Kennesaw Mountain National Battlefield Park. The park occupies 3000 acres near Marietta, Georgia. It commemorates the battle between General Joseph E. Johnston of the Confederate Army and Sherman's forces, in which Shermann outflanked his opponent and caused him to retreat to Atlanta. The earthworks are excellently preserved, and the view from the crest of Kennesaw Mountain offers superb views of the various battle areas.

Ocmulgee National Monument. Ocmulgee National Monument adjoins Macon. It contains the most impressive Indian mounds and archeological remains in the Southeast. Six different Indian cultures, from 8000 B.C. to A.D. 1717, are known to have inhabited the area. There is also a reconstruction of a large, circular, earth-covered lodge containing a clay floor, benches around the walls, and an eagle-shaped platform that was used some nine hundred years ago.

Stone Mountain Park. This park is dedicated to Confederate soldiers and sailors. Its 3000 acres enclose Stone Mountain, a massive granite dome seven miles in circumference and rising 683 feet above the surrounding plateau. The colossal equestrian figures of General Robert E. Lee, General Stonewall Jackson, and Confederate President Jefferson Davis are carved on the mountain's steep north face. A scenic railroad and a skylift are two of the many attractions built to provide spectacular views of the area.

The Little White House. The Little White House in Warm Springs was built by President Franklin D. Roosevelt in 1932 and was the place of his death in 1945. It is now a memorial shrine. The building and 4000 acres were deeded to the state of

Georgia by the Georgia Warm Springs Foundations in 1947. A large collection of Roosevelt memorabilia are contained here.

The Okefenokee Swamp. This is one of the country's great swamp areas. It begins seven miles southeast of Waycross, Georgia, and is 660 square miles in area. Two great rivers rise here – the Suwanee ("Way Down Upon the Swanee River") and the Saint Marys. The Suwanee flows into the Gulf of Mexico, and the Saint Marys into the Atlantic Ocean. The U.S. Fish and Wildlife Service maintains a refuge here for alligators, deer, black bear, and a great variety of birds.

Georgia and Tourism

Georgia is developing travel and tourist attractions with great rapidity. Excellent highways link the state with every part of America. Welcome Centers at each major entry facilitate travel in the state, extend a welcome to visitors, and have information on thirty-seven developed state parks, twenty-one wildlife refuges, and six national historical areas.

Aside from visiting the famous scenic and historical places, which are clearly marked, many people go to Georgia for fishing and water sports on its many lakes. The state has more than 400,000 acres of recreational lakes and 40,000 smaller lakes and ponds. Deep-sea fishing off the coast is one of the great attractions. The mild temperatures permit golfing at least three hundred days a year. Excellent hotels, motels, and resorts await the tourist wherever he goes.

THE PLATES

Savannah, with Independent Presbyterian Church in background
Savannah is the oldest settlement in Georgia (1733). Beautifully planned in advance by its founder, General James Edward Oglethorpe, who provided for spacious squares, streets, parks, and gardens, Savannah is one of the most beautiful and historic cities in the South. The Independent Presbyterian Church, visible in the background, dates back to 1755 and was founded by members of the Church of Scotland. The present building was erected in 1890 after the previous one burned in 1889. It is designed after St. Martin's-in-the-Fields, in London, and its steeple is in the Christopher Wren style.

Confederate War Memorial, Brunswick
This impressive war memorial, so typical of the South, stands just outside the County Courthouse. Erected in 1902, it reads as follows: IN HONOR OF THE CONFEDERATE SOLDIERS WHO DIED TO REPEL UNCONSTITUTIONAL INVASION TO PROTECT THE RIGHTS RESERVED TO THE PEOPLE TO PERPETUATE FOREVER THE SOVEREIGNTY OF THE STATES.

General John B. Gordon Monument and Capitol Building, Atlanta
The Georgia State Capitol, constructed by Edbrooke and Burnham in 1889, was patterned after the national Capitol in Washington, D.C. There are beautiful gardens with native Georgian trees, and statues of famous Georgians surround the building. The photograph shows the equestrian statue of General John B. Gordon, first governor to occupy this capitol.

Modern recreation center, Jekyll Island
This historic resort island near Brunswick was once the favorite retreat of the

54

Vanderbilts, Morgans, Pulitzers, and Rockefellers. It is today one of the most modern beach resorts in the South. A 300-foot-wide sandy beach along nine and one half miles of oceanside is kept in perfect shape, and there are bathhouses, a beach walk, and excellent parking facilities. In addition there are facilities for golf and tennis on the island. Paved roads make all parts of the island accessible.

Masters Golf Tournament, Augusta
Augusta is the Golf Capital of Georgia. The famous Augusta National Golf Club, where the Masters Invitation Tournament is played, is only one of four excellent golf courses in Augusta. All the big-name players come here, and some duffers like former President Eisenhower, who made "Mamie's Cottage" on the edge of the golf course his vacation White House.

Charles Wickersham House, Washington, Georgia
Georgia is famous for the many white-columned houses found in cities and on plantations. Washington has many of these attractive antebellum places. The book *White Columns in Georgia* by Me-

dora Field Perkerson gives a vivid description of their history, legend, folklore, and romance.

Spring in Georgia (Blue Ridge)
Spring is Georgia's most beautiful season. The fruit trees, dogwood, and magnolia are in bloom, and the young leaves turn the dark forests a brilliant green.

Double-barreled cannon, Athens
This is a curiosity of the Civil War, constructed on the theory that two chained cannonballs could be fired at the same time. It was unworkable, because the two barrels could not be synchronized. Certainly unique in all the world, it now stands in front of the Athens City Hall.

Atlanta skyline
Atlanta, the capital of Georgia, has made a rapid transition to contemporary living, clearly symbolized by the sky-scrapers in the background of the photograph and the modern expressway in the foreground. Nevertheless, it retains great symbols of its past, such as the golden dome of the capitol building, visible in the picture.

Confederate memorial carving on Stone Mountain

The picture, taken in 1967, shows the final stages in the preparation of the world's largest sculpture as it is carved into the granite face of Stone Mountain near Atlanta. The equestrian figures of three Confederate leaders, President Jefferson Davis and Generals Robert E. Lee and Stonewall Jackson, are clearly visible. Stone Mountain, a massive dome of granite, rises 683 feet above the surrounding plateau. A part of Stone Mountain Park, it was dedicated to the memory of Confederate soldiers and sailors.

Savannah skyline

The picture shows the old part of the city with the Independent Presbyterian Church and a few modern office buildings and hotels in the background. To the left can be seen the bridge over the Savannah River.

Cotton pickers

Cotton, the state's major agricultural crop, provides the raw material for Georgia's giant textile industries.

Wren's Nest, Atlanta

Wren's Nest, the former home of Joel Chandler Harris, is now a memorial to the creator of Uncle Remus and Br'er Rabbit. It is situated at 1050 Gordon Street, S.W. Its name derives from a wren's nest built in the mailbox. Harris mounted another box so as not to disturb the bird.

Fort Pulaski National Monument

Seventeen miles east of Savannah, the National Monument includes Cockspur and McQueens Islands at the mouth of the Savannah River. This historic fortification, as shown in the picture, with its rose-brick walls, is on Cockspur Island and is one of the best-preserved coastal fortifications of the early nineteenth century (built 1829–1847). It was preceded by Fort George (1761), which was dismantled by American patriots in 1776 during the Revolution, and by Fort Greene (1794–1795), which was swept away by a hurricane in 1804.

Into the Okefenokee Swamp, Waycross

Covering approximately 660 square miles, the Okefenokee Swamp is one of the largest swamps in the United States.

Two rivers rise within its boundaries – the Saint Marys, flowing into the Atlantic, and the romantic Suwanee River, which crosses into Florida and flows into the Gulf of Mexico. Five hundred square miles of the swamp are a National Wildlife Refuge. Guided tours, as indicated in the picture, make visits into the interior possible.

Midway Church

Midway between Savannah and Darien is the old Midway Church. Dating back to 1754, it was built by Puritan settlers as a Congregational church but was served by Presbyterian ministers. It was once the religious center for this whole rice-growing area. The present structure was built in 1792. From its congregation, which never had more than 150 members at any one time, came two signers of the Declaration of Independence – Lyman Hall and Button Gwinnett – two revolutionary generals, and a U.S. senator.

Pierce Butler Plantation, Darien

On the northern end of Butler Island, in the delta of the Altamaha River, is the old Pierce Butler plantation, one of the estates of Major Pierce Butler, a member of the Continental Congress (1787–1788). The vine-covered brick chimney in the foreground is part of an old rice mill. In the background is the Houston House.

Rose Test Gardens, Thomasville

This town is the site of many old plantations and is famous for its outstanding flower gardens. There is a rose festival and a rose show during the last week in April.

Library, University of Georgia, Athens

The University of Georgia (1785) is the oldest state-chartered university in the United States. The picture shows the Illah Dunlap Little Memorial Library, on the North Campus, which was dedicated in 1953. Mrs. Little, after whom it was named, provided a large sum of money in her will for the structure. Plans are under way for enlarging the building. The new Graduate Studies Research Center, on the South Campus, will house most of the science collections, and the new Law School Library contains many specialized collections. Altogether, the University Library includes about 800,000 volumes, and the current budget provides for more acquisitions than at any time in the history of the institution.

Chickamauga and Chattanooga National Military Park

In the northwest corner of Georgia lies this oldest and largest of military parks. Although situated mainly in Georgia, the Park extends over the border into Tennessee. It commemorates several Civil War battles that were fought for control of the city of Chattanooga.

Spanish moss at Wormsloe Plantation, Isle of Hope

Spanish moss is indigenous in the eastern part of Georgia and is found particularly on the various islands along Georgia's Atlantic coast. It produces a certain melancholy atmosphere when it frames old buildings and ruins such as are reproduced in this picture. The Wormsloe Plantation is nationally famous for its beautiful gardens – and also for the fact that it has been for more than two hundred years, since its construction, in the hands of the same family. These are descendants of Noble Jones, who received a grant of five hundred acres from the Georgia Trustees in 1733, soon after the colony was founded.

National Cemetery, Andersonville

Here are the graves of more than 12,400 Union soldiers who died in the overcrowded prison of Andersonville (called Camp Sumter), one of the largest Confederate prison camps. It was built to accommodate 10,000 prisoners, but up to 33,000 were incarcerated there in 1864. Because of the crowded conditions and the shortage of food and medicine, 12,462 prisoners died in a short period. In the center of the town is a monument to Captain Henry Wirz, Confederate commandant of the Andersonville Prison. He was tried on thirteen charges of maliciously conspiring to kill and torture prisoners and was hanged in Washington, D.C., on November 10, 1865. Carved into this monument, which was erected by the Daughters of the Confederacy, is the following quotation from a speech by Jefferson Davis: "When time shall have softened passion and prejudice, when reason shall have stripped the mask of misrepresentation, then justice holding evenly her scales will require much of past censure and praise to change places."

Mountain scenery near Young Harris
Some of the finest mountain scenery of
Georgia is around Young Harris, partic-
ularly as viewed looking south over the
Chatuge State Park to Georgia's highest
point, the Brasstown Bald (4,784 feet).

Birthplace of Georgia's foremost poet,
Sidney Lanier, Macon
This modest dwelling on High Street was
the home of Georgia's best-known poet,
Sidney Lanier (1842–1881).

In the mountains near Clayton
Clayton, in the middle of the Chattahoochee National Forest, is an ideal
summer resort. Its mountain scenery, with
waterfalls and numerous lakes, is most
romantic. In the vicinity, north of Clayton, is Black Rock Mountain State Park,
which covers 1,447 acres, and Black
Rock peak (3,800 feet). There are many
other mountains, such as Rabun Bald
(4,663 feet) and Screamer Mountain
(2,995 feet), named after an Indian who
ran screaming to the mountain during the
Cherokee Removal. Black Rock and
Pinnacle Mountain are centers of the
square dances, once again popular, per-
formed by the mountaineers.

Country church (Harmony Baptist Church)
near Blue Ridge
Common sights in Georgia are the
country churches situated along the highways for the use of the farmers and their
help. The photograph shows a picturesque set-up near Blue Ridge with a
little cemetery in the foreground. The area
here was once a stronghold of the
Cherokee Indians.

Walled Garden (1820) of Owens Thomas
House, Savannah
Typical of the beautiful gardens of the
old Savannah homes is the walled garden
of the Owens Thomas House, one of the
finest examples of English Regency
architecture. The house was finished in
1819 and the garden was created in 1820.
The plants that are now found in the
garden are descended from those that were
growing there when the Marquis de
Lafayette was a guest at the house in
1825. He was very fond of walking in
this garden.

Saint Marys
This is an old sea town at the mouth of
the Saint Marys River. Fishing boats, old
wooden houses, and fishnets drying in the

sun make it look like something from an old Dutch painting. Saint Marys has a history going back to the time when it was an Indian village. French Huguenots who had settled here in 1562 called the river the Seine. When the English occupied the area, they named it Saint Marys Parish (1763). After the American Revolution, the town was laid out under the name of St. Patrick, but in 1792, the town and the river were finally renamed Saint Marys.

St. Simon's Island; the Old Christ Church (1736)

This historic church was founded in 1736 by John and Charles Wesley, who established Methodism. They preached to the colonists and to the friendly Indians under a big oak tree, which still stands in the churchyard. The present structure, which is surrounded by the graves of early settlers and soldiers, was built by Anson Green Phelps Dodge, Jr., as a memorial to his wife (1884).

Savannah Beach

The Atlantic Coast of Georgia is blessed with beautiful white-sand beaches from the Golden Isles around Brunswick (St. Simon's, Jekyll, and Sea Islands) to the beaches east of Savannah. The picture shows Savannah Beach on historic Tybee Island. This is a delightful resort and has a beautiful beach, shown in the photograph. There are also boating and fishing facilities, an amusement park, and a museum of the history of the area.

The Little White House in Warm Springs

This was built by President Franklin D. Roosevelt in 1932, in the center of the health resort, in order that he might take care of his own affliction, infantile paralysis. He died here on April 12, 1945.

Warm Springs was discovered by Savannah residents who were fleeing a yellow-fever epidemic in the early nineteenth century. It soon became a health resort because of its spring waters, which had a constant temperature of 88 degrees. In 1832 there was a village here. National prominence came when Franklin D. Roosevelt started to visit here in 1925 after suffering a bout with infantile paralysis four years before. The Warm Springs Foundation offers a comprehensive program for the evaluation and care of the physically handicapped. The Little White House and 4000 acres of land were deeded in 1947 to the State of Georgia in memory of the late president. It is open to the public.

Juliette Gordon Low birthplace, Savannah

Situated at 142 Bull Street, this house, built in 1831, is now maintained by the Girl Scouts of America as a memorial to their founder, Juliette Gordon Low (1860–1927), and as a museum of historical memorabilia of Girl Scouting. It is a fine example of English Regency architecture and is open to the public.

Fort Frederica

This national monument is on St. Simon's Island. Construction on it began in 1736 under General Oglethorpe, and it became one of the mightiest British fortresses in America. It was important in the War with Spain (1739–1743). Near the fort occurred the battle of Bloody Marsh, where the British finally and completely cut off the Spanish occupation of Georgia.

PANORAMA-BOOKS

Editor Hans Andermann